Published by: Spoudazo Publishing
For permissions contact: Ruth@SpoudazoPublishing.com

Scripture quotations are from The ESV® Bible (The Holy Bible, English Standard Version®), © 2001 by Crossway, a publishing ministry of Good News Publishers. Used by permission. All rights reserved.

This publication is designed to provide accurate and authoritative information in regard to the subject matter covered. It is sold with the understanding that neither the author nor the publisher is engaged in rendering legal, investment, accounting or other professional services. While the publisher and author have used their best efforts in preparing this book, the advice and strategies contained herein may not be suitable for your situation. You should consult with a professional when appropriate.

Cover Design by: Ruth Brasch
Illustrations by: Ruth Brasch (except where noted)
Edited by Lindsay Lewchuk
First edition 2026

Comb Bound ISBN: 979-8-9944723-0-9
Paperback ISBN: 979-8-9944723-4-7
EPUB ISBN: 979-8-9944723-2-3

TABLE OF CONTENTS

INTRODUCTION & ACKNOWLEDGEMENTS

This book began because I needed to pick a study curriculum for the women's ministry at my church. I wanted a combination of study instruction and questions that would help with walking through the book of James.

Thank you:

To my husband, Clint, for encouraging me to follow the Lord's leading and write this study.

To my pastor, Dan Shunk, for the hermeneutics study outline and encouragement to follow through with writing this study.

To my friend Lindsay Lewchuck and my mother, Louise Morton, for proofreading and editing this book.

WHY DO WE STUDY THE BIBLE?

If you've been in a church for any length of time, you've probably been repeatedly instructed to study the Bible. At least, I hope your church is encouraging Bible study! But, aside from being told "study," have you been taught *how* to study?

There's many reasons for the study of the Bible as Christians; some for our own benefit and protection, some for the corporate benefit of the Body of Christ. Jesus said, "If you love Me, you will keep my commandments" (John 14:15). But how can we keep His commandments (or instructions) if we don't know what they are? Additionally, though I wish it weren't so, people in power love to claim they are following Christ and then add on religious requirements that Jesus never gave. When Jesus spoke of the Pharisees (religious rulers) in Matthew 23:4 He said that "They tie up heavy burdens, hard to bear, and lay them on people's shoulders, but they themselves are not willing to move them with their finger…" We see this today, don't we? "Church" leaders who lay on their congregations rules that never came from Christ.

I want you to know what Jesus actually said so you can obey the commands of Christ and to be free from the requirements of man. Galatians 5:1 says "For freedom Christ has set us free; stand firm therefore, and do not submit again to a yoke of slavery." Studying God's word will significantly help you understand what God asks of us and the gifts that He has given us.

Additionally, we are called to "…honor Christ the Lord as holy, always being prepared to make a defense to anyone who asks you for a reason for the hope that is in you; yet do it with gentleness and respect" (1 Peter 3:15b). If you've ever been asked a hard question about what you believe or been approached with a "Hey, you're a Christian, right? Does the Bible really say…?" Style question and felt unprepared to answer, learning to correctly understand and interpret the Word of God will prepare you to answer. That word "defense" is the Greek word *apologia*, which is where we get the English word "apologetics." While this booklet will not be focused on apologetics, or the skill of giving a reasonable answer for what you believe, my hope is that as you increase in the knowledge of biblical faith that you will become more comfortable answering others about your beliefs.

Finally, we study the Bible so we can know God in a relational aspect. Just as we spend time with our friends and begin to know them better - their likes and dislikes, favorite foods, how they'll respond to jokes, etc. Prayerfully spending time in God's Word will increase the closeness of your relationship with Him. Knowing God is the whole point. God created Adam and Eve for fellowship with Him in the Garden of Eden; they walked and talked with Him daily. We don't have that anymore, but we do have His Word and can know Him through it.

So, what will this study of the Book of James look like? I'll begin by providing some context and resources for you as you study; it's important to remember that the Bible was not written to modern Americans or by modern Americans - the inspired Word of God, inerrant in its autographs (original documents) was written by men as God inspired them. "...no prophecy of Scripture comes from someone's own interpretation. For no prophecy was ever produced by the will of man, but men spoke from God as they were carried along by the Holy Spirit." (1 Peter 2: 20b-21). Therefore, it's important that we look at the original language the scripture was written in for clarity.

I don't know about you, but I don't personally speak or read fluent Koine Greek (the original language of the New Testament), so I need to check with experts who do for interpretation and explanation sometimes! This is part of what I'll be encouraging for you as well, but with a caveat: interpretation is just that - someone reading the Word of God and telling you what they think the point is. Humans are fallible and I encourage you to not just pick one person whose opinion you accept - always read multiple sources and find those whose views reliably line up with the person of God that we meet in His word.

Each chapter will involve reading, writing down your own observations and notes, and then working through study questions. For some sections I've provided Greek translations and/or QR codes that link to reference materials. For other sections, I've left it up to you to research in the areas where you need more information. There are resources listed in the Hermeneutics overview that you can use to help your study. This can seem daunting if you've never used external research sources, but I promise that they payoff of added understanding will be more than worth it!

As you work through this book, you'll find that it's simply divided into chapters. You may want to work through an entire chapter at once, or just a few questions. Each chapter starts with an encouragement that you take time to focus your heart in prayer before the Lord before you begin study as well as focus on the overarching themes of the entire chapter. Regardless of your pace, if you don't finish the whole chapter, remember to start with prayer again when you pick up this book again, always focusing your mind and heart on Christ and asking the Holy Spirit for understanding.

I hope you'll enjoy studying the book of James with me!

Ruth

HERMENEUTICS OVERVIEW

Outline in standard text by Dan Shunk
Expansion and explanation in italics by Ruth Brasch

. . . .

Many people misunderstand what is written in the Bible. We can see this clearly just by listening to how it is discussed among people - if you asked 20 random people on the street about a passage in the Bible, you'd likely get 20 different answers. The world today wants to tell us that everyone can be right - "your truth" and "my truth" are phrases that are used regularly in conversation, but we know that truth is not subjective and God did not write the Bible in order to confuse us. 1 Corinthians 14:33 says that God is not the author of confusion.

Interpretation can be right or wrong *and people can make mistakes. I encourage you to take the study tools that are presented in this book and make a habit of studying and checking what is told to you. Check my statements against the Bible, check the statements you hear in sermons against the Bible - don't just take someone's word for it.*

Why don't people study God's Word?

One reason could be that they don't think it's relevant to their situation, don't know good reading techniques, *or struggle with reading. 54% of adults in the USA read below a 6th grade reading level[1] and the Bible is written at a 7th-12th grade reading level[2] which means that the majority of people in the USA will need some sort of help to learn to study the Bible. If that's you, please don't be embarrassed - the Bible IS for you! Reading the Bible and understanding it is not out of reach.*

We're a visual culture *that has become very dependent on videos, step by step explanations, and someone else thinking for us. Look at how study has*

---

[1] *https://www.thenationalliteracyinstitute.com/2024-2025-literacy-statistics*

[2] *https://www.christianbook.com/page/bibles/about-bibles/bible-translation-reading-levels?*

changed even in the short time period that AI has become easily accessible for the public. Rather than study for themselves, students will have AI write papers for them. Some pastors are having AI help research and write their sermons[3], generate bizarre visuals for their congregations[4], or even give spiritual advice[5] (yes, really), and some teachers are heavily leaning on AI to help them write their lessons, create assignments, and even check if their students are using AI.

Have you heard the phrase "if he wanted to he would" when when speaking about relationships? An older equivalent phrase is "where there's a will, there's a way." People may think they don't have time to study the Bible, but the reality is that we make time for what we find most important. If we have a true desire to study the Bible, we'll find a way to make it happen. This could be audio Bible study, memorization, or quick bible studies on an app interspersed with in depth study. Not every day needs to have hours of in depth study. Jesus taught His disciples to pray "give us this day our daily bread."

Some may not prioritize Bible study because they doubt the Bible is true. We must approach study of the Bible by knowing, by faith, that the Bible is infallible in its original documents and the only infallible source for knowing God (which is eternal life). The reason I emphasize "in its original documents" is because everything else is a translation by humans who are doing their very best to accurately convey meaning. You will find churches who claim to be KJV only churches, claiming that you must read from the King James Version in order to read the Bible accurately. I'd encourage you to pick a word-for-word translation (more about that a bit) that is phrased in a way you can comfortably comprehend, and begin reading there. Just as

---

[3] https://www.yahoo.com/news/chatgpt-pulpit-meet-okc-pastor-104549360.html

[4] https://churchleaders.com/news/1108715-charlie-kirks-ai-resurrection-digital-grief-rns.html

[5] https://www.nbcnews.com/news/world/deus-machina-swiss-church-installs-ai-jesus-connect-digital-divine-rcna182973

the Holy Spirit was active in the writing of the Bible (2 Peter 1:21), the Holy Spirit teaches us and helps us with understanding as we read, even if the translation isn't perfect (1 Corinthians 2:14).

Look at the benefits of studying the Bible:
You'll grow from spiritual babies to an adult (2 Peter 2:2, Hebrews 5:11-14), you'll be equipped to fulfill God's purposes (2 Timothy 3:16-17), and you'll experience the joy of discovery *and your relationship with God will grow.*

Everyone approaches the Bible with a built-in bias.
Bias means that our upbringing, the religious environment in which we were raised, our previous instruction or study, etc. all impact how we view the world and, by extension, the Bible. An important part of studying the Bible is to examine the history of the book and the intent of the author so we can understand correctly what the meaning of the scripture is. God put every detail into Scripture intentionally and if we allow our biases to add or remove meaning from the Bible, we're in the wrong. As you study, be open to the possibility that you've previously been taught incorrectly or have learned things about God that aren't accurate to what He tells us.

Why do people misinterpret the Bible?
Some lack faith in things to come (John 12:16, 13:7) Some seek to make doctrine when the Bible is subtle or silent, *meaning that they create rules that God hasn't made or say that God has clearly spoken on a topic when He hasn't. Some lack understanding of what the Bible is actually saying.*

What are the goals of studying the Bible?
To understand the intent of the author (Psalm 19:7, Psalm 119:130) *which means we need to study who the author is, when he was writing, historical events and context at the time, how the book has traditionally been interpreted, and what the stated purpose of the book is.*
Jesus thought Scripture was clear *when teaching, He used the phrase "have you not read..." when explaining doctrine and life application. This means He assumed that people would not only be continually studying the Scripture but also be thinking critically about what it means.*

For Christians, the Scripture should produce spiritual transformation. Engaging with the scriptures with both your intellect and heart, with the aid of the Holy Spirit, should produce change in your life. (I Corinthians 2:14, Romans 12:2, Ephesians 4:23, Psalm 119:11)

BIBLE STUDY TIPS AND TECHNIQUES

Now that we've established why we want to study the Bible and the fact that interpretation matters, we're going to move into some techniques and tips for studying.

P.R.E.S.S. - Pray, Read, Establish a time, Study, Share (Deut 6:6-7)
This acronym can help you remember a routine for study. Please notice how it's similar to any other routine - don't just assume you'll have time to study the Bible if you don't make time.
P*ray before you read and ask the Holy Spirit for understanding and clarity.*
R*ead the Bible at the*
E*stablished time*
S*tudy beyond what you see on the surface and then*
S*hare with a friend and check for feedback - the body of Christ is here for a reason!*

There are many Bible translations out there, so how do you know which one to choose? Let's learn a little bit more about the differences in translations with this graphic[6] and some more details on the next page.

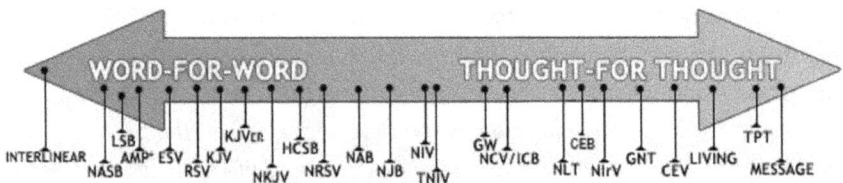

WORD-FOR-WORD   THOUGHT-FOR-THOUGHT

INTERLINEAR   LSB   AMP   ESV   KJV   KJVᴇʀ   HCSB   NAB   NIV   GW   CEB   GNT   LIVING   TPT
      NASB   RSV   NKJV   NRSV   NJB   TNIV   NCV/ICB   NLT   NIrV   CEV   MESSAGE

---

[6] https://www.christianbook.com/page/bibles/about-bibles/about-translations? event=Bibles|1005256

Literal / Formal / Word-for-Word Translations - *This approach seeks to represent the original Greek and Hebrew in a more word-for-word manner and preserve—as far as possible—original word order, grammar, and syntax.[7]* KJV, NKJV, NASB, LSB, ESV, RSV/NRSV, CSB/HCSB.

For study, choose one of these first!

Dynamic Equivalence- *These translations seek to strike a balance between Word-for-Word and Thought-for-Thought Paraphrases. They are sometimes more literal, sometimes more colloquial or conversational depending on the subject and text.[8]* NIV/TNIV, NLT, CEV

Paraphrases - *This approach is more concerned with putting meaning of the passage in a colloquial language familiar to the reader. This type of translation seeks to render the ideas of the original text as accurately as possible in the target language (like English).[9]*
(The Message and The Living Bible)

Dynamic Equivalence translations and Paraphrases can be used as tools to aid understanding, if desired, but not for study translations since they are less concerned with accuracy.

Regarding Study Bibles
Some are helpful – but remember the inspiration stops at the line, *which means that when you see explanations added in, they're the (hopefully) well-thought out opinions of a human, not the inspired Word of God.*

Other Tools
Concordances - *A concordance lists every time a word is used in the Bible in a specific translation. This can be helpful for cross referencing and finding clarity because you can see where else a word is used.*

---

[7] *ibid*

[8] *ibid*

[9] *ibid*

Dictionaries - *For looking up English words you don't know.*

Lexicons & Interlinear Bibles - *A lexicon is essentially a dictionary of a foreign language. It helps to explain the words themselves. An interlinear Bible shows the original text next to the English translation - think of bilingual Bibles with Spanish on one side and English on the other.*

Commentaries - These are *someone's* opinion, some good, some bad. *It can be helpful to read how others have understood the Bible, especially those who have studied for a long time or received a good education in how to properly interpret, but the Word of God is for everyone!*

All of these can be found in physical form or on websites and applications such a E-Sword, the Bible app, Blue Letter Bible, etc.
Methods of Study and Topics
1. Choose a section of text - *Some prefer to work chronologically through the Bible, some pick a book like we are in this study of James.*

2. *Choose* a subject- *This might look like studying the miracles of Jesus across the gospels, or the interactions of the early church. Instead of just looking at a single book of the Bible, you would look for all the places this topic is mentioned and study through them.*

3. Character Study - *Choose a specific person and learn more about them. Use historical resources to help you better understand who they were and their impact.*

Understanding the Intent of the Author
One of our goals of study is to understand the intent of the author and be transformed. Getting familiar *with* the word pictures and culture *of the Bible as a whole and also of the specific book* will help you see past the words and into the realities that they convey. *Our feelings exist for a reason, but we are not to be driven by our feelings, nor do we base our interpretation of scripture on the way it makes us feel.*

When you feel uncomfortable during your study time, it's time to examine the cause: whether it's because what the Bible says conflicts with culture, with our current morality and ethics, or because we are misinterpreting what we're reading.

Types of Literature in the Bible
You wouldn't pick up a novel and expect to use it as a guidebook to a foreign country, would you? When Shakespeare famously wrote Romeo and Juliet, he wrote, "But soft! What light through yonder window breaks? It is the east, and Juliet is the sun." (Romeo and Juliet, Act 2, Scene 2)[10]. Obviously Juliet is not literally the sun, but is being compared to it to demonstrate how enamored teenaged Romeo is with her. We know this because of the type of literature that Romeo and Juliet is as well as the fact that common sense and logic dictate that a teenager is not literally a flaming ball of gas in space.

Similarly, knowing what type of literature you're reading in the Bible is immensely helpful for understanding.
Use the acronym LAMP to help you remember.

Literal
Allegorical
Moral (wisdom)
Personal application

Using the LAMP method

Literal *Start here. If you read a portion of scripture and it contains an easily understandable, not-qualified instruction (in other words, there aren't conditions attached to it), take it at face value. When Jesus says, "Love your neighbor as yourself," don't look for another interpretation or conditions in which you don't need to love others. Love your neighbor!*

---

[10] *http://shakespeare.mit.edu/romeo_juliet/full.html*

Allegorical
Allegory - Use of characters, settings, or events to represent a larger or deeper meaning. e.g. using Aslan, the lion in The Chronicles of Narnia, to represent Jesus. We know he is meant to represent Christ because we can see scenes of his crucifixion and resurrection played out in The Lion, The Witch, and the Wardrobe and descriptions of him being the "son of the Emperor-Over-the-Sea (God)" in The Magician's Nephew.

In Galatians 4:21-31, Paul uses the allegory of Abraham's wives to explain how and why we do not need to follow the old law anymore. Read through that passage and see how it helps your understanding of allegory.

We should interpret the text as allegory only when the *it* says to; *if we interpreted, for example, the creation narrative in Genesis 1-2 as an allegory or metaphor, our entire understanding of the rest of the Bible and the nature of God changes. Genesis 1:1 says,"In the beginning, God created the heavens and the earth." We don't need to introduce other interpretation to that.*

Moral / Personal Application
When Jesus told parables, *He was very clear about it, or the writers of the Bible added clarity. They'll say; "Then He spoke a parable to them..." (Luke 18:1a) or Matthew 13:18, "Hear the parable of the sower..."*

A couple definitions
*Simile - Comparing two things using the words "like" or "as" in the comparison. (e.g. cool **as** a cucumber, she ran **like** the wind in that race)*

We see these all the time in the parables and teachings of Jesus. For example, "He said therefore, "What is the kingdom of God like? And to what shall I compare it? It is **like** a grain of mustard seed that a man took and sowed in his garden, and it grew and became a tree, and the birds of the air made nests in its branches." (Luke 13:18-19)

Metaphor - Using one thing to explain or represent another. For example, "Judah is a lion's cub…" (Genesis 49:9a)[11] Obviously Judah is not literally a lion, but we can understand from this metaphor what Jacob is trying to say about his child and the future of the tribe of Judah.

Overall Study Advice

1. Come to know the obscure passages based on the clear ones - If you're having trouble interpreting a section of the Bible, see if there are other related passages that can help add clarity. This is where interlinear helps or study bibles can be really useful - they'll list related scriptures for you.

2. Keep a list of your unanswered questions – you'll answer them soon and writing them down helps with processing and figuring out what your actual question is. The Questions & Answers section at the end of this book is a great spot to keep study questions. Remember to list answers when you find them as well!

3. Don't rush through this study; if you mix it up, problems compound quickly. In other words, take the time to ensure that you've worked through the details. Every detail has been put in the Scriptures intentionally and you **can** find the answer!

Interpreting and Interacting with the Bible

Interpretation can be right or wrong. Despite what society says, there **is** a wrong way to interpret the Bible and God does have a specific intent behind what is written. It's important to note, however, that we are fallible. Expecting that you will **always** have the correct interpretation and that others are **always** wrong is just silly.

---

[11] https://www.wordnik.com/words/metaphor

What do we do when we come to a passage we don't agree with?

1. Check for understanding. Use available resources to ensure that we are correctly interpreting what the Bible says.
> *a. Use interlinear references*
> *b. Cross reference with related verses*
> *c. Use a concordance, dictionary, or commentary*
> *d. Ask a spiritual mentor, like your pastor*

2. Figure out why you don't agree with what you're reading. Does it conflict with your biases (how you were raised, the morality of the culture you live in, etc?) or does it not make sense to you in light of other things you've read in the Bible?
> *a. If it doesn't mesh with the culture or your biases, you need to change.*
> *b. If it seems to conflict with what you've previously read or understood about God, see number 1.*

3. Change if necessary

CAUTION: *If you don't understand what you're reading, don't agree with it, or the passage contains a miracle, pause before deciding that change is necessary and do some further study.*

People interpret Scriptures *in a variety of ways. As previously mentioned, our cultural understandings or biases can influence how we understand scripture. The goal is to understand the author's intention, not our current reading of it or how we feel about it.*

If we don't understand or find a passage of the Bible confusing, our first step should be to assume that **we** *have not understood correctly and need more information or clarity. The Bible is not wrong. Hebrews 4:12 says, "For the word of God is living and active, sharper than any two-edged sword, piercing to the division of soul and of spirit, of joints and of marrow, and discerning the thoughts and intentions of the heart."*

Steps to take when studying the Bible

1. Keep your analysis simple
2. Isolate the essential moral teaching being taught
3. List the known cross references
4. Note other doctrines are clearly being taught
5. To understand the Old Testament, put Jesus in the middle of everything (Luke 24, Acts 8)

Before Studying, Find Out the Following:

Who - wrote it, spoke it, heard it.
We need to know not only the author, but also the intended audience. What was the culture of the people who would read the epistles and hear them read aloud? Who was the author and how would that impact his writing?

What - know all the nouns. *A noun is a person, place, thing, or idea. A Proper Noun is a specific person, place, thing, or idea. For example, "man" is a general person. It could be any man, but "Clint" is a specific man, so Clint is a proper noun. Church is a common noun, but Notre Dame Cathedral is a proper noun.*

Scan the QR code if you need more information on nouns and how you can identify them in the text.

Where - what do we know about the place currently, historically, personally? *Since names of places change over time, it's important to understand where these places were located historically. What was the culture like? Have you been to one of these places?*

Why - understand the language, is it a cultural thing - *Different languages have different rules, expressions, idioms, etc. Learning more about the language itself and the cultures that used it can greatly add to our understanding of what is written.*

Did you know that idioms don't translate? If you say, "mad as a wet hen" or "raining cats and dogs" to a non-native English speaker, you'll have to explain what you mean.

When – visualize what's happening, know the atmosphere *- For example, Philippians was written while Paul was in prison, which means that Paul wrote "rejoice in the Lord always, again I say rejoice" (Philippians 4:4) while he was imprisoned. Knowing the setting and circumstances of the author can greatly impact your interpretation and application.*

How – know the verbs, what's the literary form (poetry, comedy, narrative) *- Verbs are actions or states of being. Running, jumping, praising, speaking, loving, and sitting are all action verbs, but "is" "are" "am" "was" "were" are being verbs. They tell us whether some thing is happening right now or happened in the past and how many people it is happening to.*

For example, the phrase "I were sitting" will sound incorrect to your ear as a native English speaker. Do you know why? In English, verbs must be linked to the number of people as well as the state of being. You may have seen conjugation charts in school as a child and hated or not understood them, but let me show you why grammar is so important!

Conjugating being verbs:
1st person means 1 person speaking about themselves
2nd person means 1 person speaking about someone else (about the second person)
3rd person is multiple people speaking about themselves as a group or about another group.

For example:
Present tense (something happening right now)
Singular (about one person)
1st person: I am
2nd person: you are
3rd person: he/she/it is

Present tense (something happening right now)
Plural (about more than one person)
1st person: We are
2nd person: You are
3rd person: They are
*Note: it is becoming increasingly popular in current culture to use "they" as a 3rd person singular pronoun when the gender of the person being referred to is unknown, in an attempt to remove binary gendered language (male and female only), but you will not find this in the Bible. If you see "they" in the Bible, it is always referring to the third person plural.

So, why is understanding this necessary?

Examples of plural language in the Bible that impacts theology:

Genesis 1:1 - in the beginning, Elohim created the heavens and the earth. "Elohim" is the plural form of the Hebrew word for God. What does it indicate that the plural form of a word, which would usually indicate multiple gods is being used to indicate the one true God? It aims us toward understanding the triune nature of God. From the very beginning, God has been triune in nature.

Genesis 1:26 - "Let US make man in OUR image, after OUR likeness…" (emphasis mine). Again, right from the beginning, studying the grammar shows God speaking in a plural form. To whom is He speaking? Does it matter? It does, because it established the triune nature of God. Further on in scripture, God will tell Moses that he is One and should be taught to all of Israel that way.

Today, throughout the word, the statement of Deuteronomy 6:4 is repeated by Jews throughout the world every day: "Hear, O Israel: The Lord our God, the Lord is one."

Since we know that God does not lie (Titus 1:2) and that God is the same as He has always been (Hebrews 13:8), that means that God is both plural and one at the same time.

Can't wrap your head around it? That's ok! Sometimes it's enough to hold the truth without full understanding.

Look for patterns
When we read books, we tend to look for the theme of the book. When reading the Bible, there are multiple themes and essentials that are covered repeatedly, so here are a few tips for finding them.

Look for patterns by seeing what is emphasized using textual clues. Terms, people, incidents, etc may be repeated to prove a point. New Testament authors quoting from the Old Testament is a good example of this.

Text order and contents my provide emphasis as well. If you're reading a book of the Bible and the text is flowing well and then suddenly you notice something changes - the author seems to get a little off topic for a minute (I'm looking at you, Paul) and you wonder why that information has been placed in the middle of the rest, look at what's being said.

As your Bible study grows, your knowledge of Bible will begin to create connections for you. Just as study Bibles have notes about connected passages of Scripture, your brain will begin to create those or you. You'll begin to notice cause and effect, repetition, emphasis, themes, and more.

Application
You'll notice that application is the last step. The reason for this is that we need to understand what we're supposed to do before we begin doing it. We're surrounded by people who choose their own standards, pick and choose little bits of the Bible, or try to make Jesus in their own image.

You'll hear application before analysis happen all the time in conversations once you start listening for it. My favorite example is Philippians 4:13 - "I can do all things through Christ who strengthens me."

This verse has been slapped onto bumper stickers, instagram posts, and cross stitched wall hangings where people use it to tell themselves they can get through anything. If you go back and read the context, Paul was in prison saying he's learned to be content with every situation. That's wildly different from a photo of a rock climber with Philippians 4:13 transposed on it!

The Bible was written to transform our lives. *As you'll see in our study in James, action and application are very much a part of faith. James 1:22 says "But be doers of the word, and not hearers only, deceiving yourselves." That's a pretty clear instruction!*

When you study God's Word, it gets into your heart and mind and changes you. You'll act differently, think differently, and make choices you wouldn't have before. You'll be "transformed by the renewal of your mind, that by testing you may discern what is the will of God, what is good and acceptable and perfect." (Romans 12:2b)

Application can look different depending on the situation, person, and interpretation. Acts 17:21-26 shows us believers from a variety of backgrounds applying the scripture in different ways. Those who had been raised with a Jewish background saw Jesus as the promised Messiah (He is) and thus the ultimate fulfillment of the Law, so they behaved in accordance with their culture and customs.

On the other hand, Gentile (non-Jewish) believers were told "But as for the Gentiles who have believed, we have sent a letter with our judgment that they should abstain from what has been sacrificed to idols, and from blood, and from what has been strangled, and from sexual immorality." (Acts 17:25) Does the essence of following Christ change? No. The moral teaching was to worship Christ. It's simply explained differently and may look visually different depending on the cultural understanding of the one practicing it.

If you've never experienced a church culture aside from the one you're in, or have never listened to believers outside of your culture, you're missing out on a depth and wealth of knowledge. Assuming that your culture is the only or best way to express faith in Christ will leave you with a narrow, ethnocentric view of God.

When applying scripture to your life and life circumstances, begin with yourself before others. Find the moral or instruction in scripture. For example, if you read Matthew 22:36-40 "Teacher, which is the great commandment in the Law?" And he said to him, "You shall love the Lord your God with all your heart and with all your soul and with all your mind. This is the great and first commandment. And a second is like it: You shall love your neighbor as yourself. On these two commandments depend all the Law and the Prophets." And your immediate response is "My Mom is so rude to people and she definitely does't love her neighbors!" STOP. First ask the Lord to handle your heart with relation to how you're loving your Mom.

> Application note: I'm NOT saying that if someone is harming you that you just need to pray about it and submit to it. That's a gross misuse of the scripture that occurs in way too many situations. You do NOT need to maintain contact or relationship, with an abuser or someone who is continually harming you in some way. You're not a bad wife, daughter, or friend to protect yourself from being harmed.

Often, I've been annoyed to find that the problem I was praying about was solved when I submitted to the Lord in obedience to the instructions in His Word. "Lord, this person at work is annoying me, please make them stop!" Guess who ends up changing? It's you. The Lord will help you to see them through His eyes - as a beautiful and valuable creation of His.

Once you've applied it to yourself, you're then applying in concentric circles outward: to those in your household, family, close friends, church, social settings, etc. It's not so import that you follow the exact order that I'm specifying as that you understand internal change should be the priority and that the Scripture is a lens through which we view family, society, friends, etc, but we are not always able to change them. Sometimes you will be an agent of change in those locations simply by your lifestyle and how you speak of and relate to God.

Once you've read, take time to pray about what you've read, studied, and want to apply to your life. Application isn't always easy, so keep the Word of God close to you - memorize scripture, write it down on notecards, whatever you need to do! You can even write the verses on one side and the application on the other and carry them around to remind you of the application if need be.

BACKGROUND ON THE BOOK OF JAMES

Author: Most scholars agree that the James who wrote the book of James was the biological half brother of Jesus, meaning he was the son of Mary and Joseph. In Galatians 2:9 he is named as a "pillar" of the early church, meaning he had a position of authority and his opinion and knowledge were respected.

Date: "The book of James was probably written between AD 48 and 52, though nothing in the epistle suggests a more precise date. James's death in AD 62 or 66 means the epistle was written before this time."[12]

Here's a brief timeline[13] of the early church to give you a good idea of what was happening around this time, up to and including the death of James so you can have context for his writing of the book regardless of whether it was 45 AD or later. "C." Means "circa," which stands for "about," which is in there to indicate that we don't have exact dates for these events.

c.29/33: Crucifixion, resurrection, and ascension of Jesus
c.33/37: Stephen becomes first martyr
c. 33/37: Paul converted on the road to Damascus
c.45/46: Epistle of James is first New Testament book written
c.46/47: Barnabas and Paul leave on their first missionary journey
c.49/50: Jerusalem Council
c.50/51: Paul launches his second missionary journey
c.52: Thomas spreads the gospel to India
c.53/54: Paul launches his third missionary journey
c.62/64: Gospel of Mark is first Gospel written
64: Great fire of Rome, Emperor Nero blames Christians
c.66/68: Peter and Paul martyred under Nero's persecution

---

[12] *CSB Holy Land Illustrated Bible (Nashville, Tennessee: Holman Bible Publishers, 2020) 1794.*

[13] *https://www.theologyfortherestofus.com/christian-history-timeline-most-influential-events-in-church-history#aa*

Location of Original Readers: Various location. James 1:1 says the letter is "to the twelve tribes dispersed abroad." Why did this happen?

Acts 8:1-4 tells us:
"And Saul approved of his [Stephen's] execution.
And there arose on that day a great persecution against the church in Jerusalem, and they were all scattered throughout the regions of Judea and Samaria, except the apostles. Devout men buried Stephen and made great lamentation over him. But Saul was ravaging the church, and entering house after house, he dragged off men and women and committed them to prison. Now those who were scattered went about preaching the word.

So, the Gospel of Christ was being spread because of persecution. Because the persecution was so intense in Jerusalem, many believers who had, for a time, enjoyed the large common fellowship of Christians, began to move and travel to other locations for their own safety. In Acts alone, we see that they travelled to Samaria (Acts 8:5, Acts 8:9), Philip preached the Gospel to an Ethiopian (Acts 8:26-39), Paul preached in Damascus after his conversions (Acts 9:20-22), and so on until we begin to see distant missionary journeys occurring and the beginning of what we would call modern churches growing.

Scan the QR code to the right and check out Paul's missionary journeys to see all the places he went - it'll save you time from having to read them all in a list from me!

CHAPTER 1

Before you begin, take a moment to pray and ask the Holy Spirit to open your mind and heart to know Him and understand His word. In the words of Paul, "that the God of our Lord Jesus Christ, the Father of glory, may give you the Spirit of wisdom and of revelation in the knowledge of him, having the eyes of your hearts enlightened, that you may know what is the hope to which he has called you…" (Ephesians 1:17-18). I encourage you to even insert your name into that verse and pray the scripture for yourself in this way:

Lord, I ask that the God of our Lord Jesus Christ, the Father of glory, will give me the Spirit of wisdom and revelation in the knowledge of Him. Please enlighten the eyes of my heart the I may know the hope to which You called me.

Read through all of Chapter 1, just to get a feel for it.
Below, write down themes that are repeated.

We read in the introduction that James held a position of authority and prominence in the church, but how does he introduce himself in this letter?

How would you define joy (verse 2)?

What is the difference between joy and happiness? You may want to look up definitions if you aren't sure.

In verse 3 there's a word that differs by translation. "The testing of your faith produces... (steadfastness/perseverance/endurance/patience, etc) so what is the word and what does it mean? The Greek word is hypomonē (say: hoop-om-on-AY) and the definition is steadfastness, constancy, and endurance - "in the NT the characteristic of a man who is not swerved from his deliberate purpose and his loyalty to faith and piety by even the greatest trials and sufferings." (Strongs G5281).

How does the testing of our faith produce hypomonē - the ability to patiently endure even in the hardest of times and how is hypomonē different from resignation or regular endurance?

Verse 4 says that the "full effect" of hypomonē is "perfect" ness. We know that only God is perfect, so looking at the Greek again, we find that the original word is *teleios* (say: tel'-ee-os), which translates to "complete" or "of full age" in the sense that an adult is fully grown instead of being a child. How does that change your understanding of the result of suffering?

Does understanding the result of trials make them easier to endure? Why or why not?

Application note: all of us have been in the situation where knowing the outcome of the trial or that it will bring growth in us doesn't assuage the experience of pain or the suffering. For example, if your friend has lost a child or spouse, jumping right to telling them it'll refine their faith in the end is a really inappropriate response. When Jesus encountered the death of a loved one/friends grieving the loss of their brother in John 11, His response was that he felt disturbed and upset; when they took him to the grave of Lazarus, He wept. *Then,* later, they were able to discuss the spiritual implications.

Please emulate Christ as you comfort those who are currently suffering. Romans 12:15 tells us to "rejoice with those who rejoice and weep with those who weep." A well-meaning "this will strengthen your faith!" without empathy and compassion is not a Christ-like response.

Re-read verses 5-8. What impact does faith have on our requests for wisdom?

In verse 8 James refers to a double-minded man.

Scan the QR code and read the definition of double-minded (Strongs G1374) in a concordance. How does that definition change your understanding of asking for wisdom "with no doubting"?

Did you know you can ask God for faith? Some people are gifted with faith, others struggle with it, but you can always ask God to increase your faith in Him. Just remember that, as James 1:2 says, sometimes the way our faith is increased is through trials - we learn the faithfulness of God as we walk through life and see his care of us time and time again. I can tell you, from personal experience, that God can handle your questions, your doubt, your anger, and your frustration. Take a moment to pause and consider your current view of God and how you're relating to Him. Ask Him for what you need before you move on.

Re-read verses 9-11. They can feel a little bit like a deviation from the theme at first glance. How do these verses relate to the previous sections? What does being rich or poor have to do with faith in God, or the quantity of wisdom we have?

Verses 12-18 help us understand the insertion of verses 9-11. Value, in life, is not about how much money we have or our social standing, but rather in our relationship to God and how He refines and shapes us through life. Our true reward comes from a life lived in faithfulness to God.

What is the promised reward from God for those who are faithful to Him? (Verse 12)

What *is* the "crown of life"? Time to dig a little deeper and use some of our resources! Use either a Lexicon, concordance, or commentary and explain what you find.

According to verse 13, why is it impossible that temptation comes from God?

What causes our temptation?

Verse 16 employs a literary technique called "foiling." It directly contrasts two people by comparing them. In this case, our proclivity for temptation is being foiled against God's holiness. How does this impact our view of ourselves and of Him?

Despite the fact that the next chapter break has not occurred yet, how does the tone of the book of James change beginning in verse 19?

Read Verses 19-27 again. This section is an excellent example of personal application literature. James has transferred from general exhortations about the nature of God and difficulty to practical application for how we should live our lives.

In the box on the next page, write down every instruction given about our behavior. No need to write the whole verse - just a little note or abbreviation. I've done the first one!

```
Quick to hear




```

Looking at the box of instructed behavior characteristics, how many of them are things you directly struggle with?

Please know that everyone struggles. James didn't write a list of behaviors and expect that we would immediately hit the target on all of them. We all have different personalities, strengths, and weaknesses; we'll struggle with different areas of life, which is why we need the sanctifying work of the Holy Spirit as well as the support of the church.

Read 1 Corinthians 12:12-27 and then Hebrews 10:19-25. How does that impact your view of the list of behaviors that we noted above? Does it make it easier to understand that we all need to work collectively and encourage one another?

How does James describe someone who cannot control their tongue?

What is "pure and undefiled" religion, according to verse 27?

Are these definitions different that what you've previously been taught?

Read Micah 6:8. How does it reinforce the instructions in this chapter?

Before we end chapter 1, lets talk a little bit about our hearts and attitudes, because it can be very easy to focus on what we are doing and not how we are doing it.

Read 1 Corinthians 13. What must be the primary motivation and focus of our hearts while we evaluate our behaviors?

What words or descriptors does 1 Corinthians 13 use to describe those who act without love?

CHAPTER 2

Before you begin, take a moment to pray and ask the Holy Spirit to open your mind and heart to know Him and understand His word. In the words of Paul, "that the God of our Lord Jesus Christ, the Father of glory, may give you the Spirit of wisdom and of revelation in the knowledge of him, having the eyes of your hearts enlightened, that you may know what is the hope to which he has called you…" (Ephesians 1:17-18). I encourage you to even insert your name into that verse and pray the scripture for yourself in this way:

Lord, I ask that the God of our Lord Jesus Christ, the Father of glory, will give me the Spirit of wisdom and revelation in the knowledge of Him. Please enlighten the eyes of my heart the I may know the hope to which You called me.

Read through all of Chapter 2, just to get a feel for it.
Below, write down themes that are repeated.

Read verses 1-7.
Verse 1 makes a very clear statement with no qualifiers: Don't show partiality.

The word partiality, in Greek, is προσωπολημψία, transliterated as prosōpolēmpsia (say: pros-o-pol-ape-see'-ah). It's only used 3 other places in the entire Bible, so we're going to check them out!

Read Romans 2:11, Ephesians 6:9, and Colossians 3:25.
Based on these three verses, as well as the section we're working through in James, what does partiality mean and who are we behaving like if we do not show partiality?

34

Take a moment for personal reflection. Is there a person or group of people that you look down on or treat as if they are less valuable? Do you use qualifiers to justify your treatment or opinion of them, like "they deserve it" or use something they've done in the past?

Application note: please note that these are all verses about treatment by and within the church, by God to us, etc. I'm not advocating that you need to maintain contact or relationship with an abuser or someone who is continually harming you in some way.

If you are being harmed at home and need help, please tell someone you trust or call the national domestic violence hotline: 1-799-SAFE

Think for a moment about who the world promotes as worthwhile. We have people in our country who are literally called idols or are treated as if they are gods. What are the characteristics the world values in order for a person to be treated well?

What does God say about the way our minds have changed if we treat some people differently than others? (Verse 4)

Read 1 Corinthians 1:26-31. How does it relate to or round out your understanding of this passage (Verses 1-7)?

What do we know about the Kingdom of God based on Jesus's statement in Mark 9:35?

Keep these things in mind as you go through your day. The next time you see someone and your reaction is "ugh" or to look down on them, remember Hebrews 13:2, which says "Do not neglect to show hospitality to strangers, for thereby some have entertained angels unawares."

Read verses 8-13. What is the summary of these last few verses, especially as they relate to how we interact with others?

Read Verses 14-26.
Have you ever had these verses used to tell you certain actions were necessary for salvation? Write down your reaction to these verses - your initial thoughts and feelings. We don't interpret the Scripture by our feelings, but assessing them can help us understand our knowledge and responses.

Is verse 14 saying that we must perform certain actions for salvation? It might sound that way upon first reading. It's time to cross reference with some other verses about salvation and see if we can gain some clarity.

Read Ephesians 2:8-9. According to that verse, what saves us and what does not?

These two verses seem to be at odds with each other. We know that the Bible is inerrant in its original form, so lets check and see if the word for "save" is the same. I'll save you some time, but give you references so you can double check what I'm telling you - it's the same word. The Greek word is sozo, (G4982 in Strong's concordance if you want to look it up) so it's definitely the same word.

How, then, can we reconcile these two statements that seem to be opposing each other? Lets read a little further in this current section of James - it adds clarity!

Verses 15-16 give us concrete examples of a person who claims to have faith but doesn't live it out in their lifestyle.
What are the two examples given of needs that could be met as followers of Christ are living out their faith?

How does James describe faith that doesn't inspire action (verse 17)?

Verse 18 adds additional clarity for us. Read it and see if it helps you understand how James and the book of Ephesians and salvation through grace are not at odds with one another. What additional understanding did you gain?

How do you know someone cheers for a specific sports team? They wear their uniform, watch their games, attend their games, and they talk about it with every single person they know. Usually, you don't even have to ask someone if they're a fan of a certain sports team because their behavior, what they wear, how they spend their time, and what they talk about will tell you all you need to know.

In the same way, James is saying that if you claim you have faith, but your "faith" doesn't have any outward appearance of it, you might just have a religious identity, not life-changing faith. According to James, if your faith in Christ is not prompting you to feed the hungry, clothe those who need it, and ensure that the needs of others are being met, you have a shallow faith that has not yet produced change and growth in your own life.

Take a moment to do some self-reflection. Does your life have outward evidence of the inward faith you hold? If not, don't condemn yourself, but ask the Lord for strengthening of your faith and for opportunities to show his love to others by meeting their needs. Those could be physically needs, emotional needs, etc. Look at how Jesus behaved to others while He was here on this earth, then do your best to emulate it with His help. Write below a couple ways you could provide help and care for those in need. Please remember that "help" isn't necessarily financial - not all needs are!

Read Verses 19-26.
How do these additional examples emphasize the point that James was making earlier on?

How did Abraham demonstrate that he believed God?

How did Rahab demonstrate that she believed God?

The goal of this portion is not to make you feel guilty, so you immediately leave and take the entire contents of your bank account to the closest homeless shelter. Reflect on your current lifestyle. Is there a way that your actions could be used to practically share the love of God?

CHAPTER 3

Before you begin, take a moment to pray and ask the Holy Spirit to open your mind and heart to know Him and understand His word. In the words of Paul, "that the God of our Lord Jesus Christ, the Father of glory, may give you the Spirit of wisdom and of revelation in the knowledge of him, having the eyes of your hearts enlightened, that you may know what is the hope to which he has called you…" (Ephesians 1:17-18). I encourage you to even insert your name into that verse and pray the scripture for yourself in this way:

Lord, I ask that the God of our Lord Jesus Christ, the Father of glory, will give me the Spirit of wisdom and revelation in the knowledge of Him. Please enlighten the eyes of my heart the I may know the hope to which You called me.

Read through all of Chapter 3, just to get a feel for it.
Below, write down themes that are repeated.

Read verses 1-12
Why do you think the admonition that few should teach is connected to the section about controlling our speech?

Read Matthew 18:6. Do you see the connection between what Jesus said there and James' statement in verse 1 about the serious consequences of teaching incorrectly?

List below all the comparisons James uses to explain the impact our speech has on our lives. This is one place where we clearly are to interpret these as analogies. Obviously, for example, James does not think we have tongues full of physical poison.

Like a rudder steering a ship

Focus on verses 9-12. Why do you think these verses about how we use our tongues are placed right after the chapter about not showing partiality?

What do you think is the key idea in this section of verses?

James was very clear that the tongue is not tamable by us. Verse 2 says that if we could control our speech perfectly, we'd essentially be perfect. This doesn't mean there's no hope for you if you struggle with your speech, or that you're evil. We all have areas of our lives that need to be continually submitted to God for sanctification.

Read Romans 12:2. How does that impact the way that you approach your speech? What must change internally in order for an external change to appear?

With that in mind, take a moment to reflect and ask the Lord for help in the area where you struggle most with your speech.

Read Proverbs 18:21, Ephesians 4:29, Proverbs 25:11, Romans 12:18, Matthew 18:15-17. In light of these, how does God want us to speak with others and deal with conflict?

Does the continuity between multiple books of the Bible comfort you? It comforts me. I appreciate being able to read through multiple books of the Bible and see that the message is exactly the same.

Go a little further in Romans 12 and read verses 3-8 and then compare them with James 2:1-9. What do you see in common between these two passages?

Does it feel a little bit like you're going in circles or taking two steps forward and one step back to be reading in this manner? That's common! The interconnectedness of the Bible means that we don't always just read in a liner manner, but sometimes we flip back and forth between sections, compare, or end up down a little rabbit hole of interest, learning more about what we're reading.

That's the purpose of providing you with study tools at the beginning of this book! If you are working through this study and you remember something you were previously taught, or you were studying another book of the Bible recently and the Lord brings it to mind, stick a bookmark in James and go see how it relates!

Read verses 13-18. We're entering a section that compares and contrasts things. They're discussed next to each other to show the difference between them.

According to verse 13, how do you know that someone is wise or knowledgeable?

Meekness (v. 13) is the Greek word πραΰτης (transliterated: prautēs, say "prah-oo'-tace"). According to Strong's concordance (G4240), it means "mildness of disposition, gentleness of spirit, meekness."

This gentleness is listed in Galatians 5:23 as one of the fruits of the spirit.

If meekness/gentleness is a fruit of the Spirit and wisdom also come from God, how can you become one of these people who is gentle and wise?

Check out James 1:5-7 again and write your answer below.

For more about meekness/gentleness, scan this code and scroll down to see other places where it is used in the Bible. You'll be amazed!

Verse 14 shows us a contrast of the person in verse 13. What actions are the opposite of a wise man's actions?

Verses 15-16 again show one group of descriptions and verses 17-18 show their contrasts.

What does it look like when there is "wisdom" that isn't from God being put into action (verses 15-16)?

And what is the contrast (verses 17-18)?

Please notice that James does ask you to look at the behaviors in someone's life as an indication of what they value and where their priorities lie.

For extra study time, reference Matthew 7. Jesus spoke clearly about this very topic. I want to caution you, however, that maturing in understanding behaviors is not the same thing as applying your cultural rules or personal convictions to someone else.

What do I mean by that?

Check out 1 Corinthians 10:23-33. Paul is encouraging the Corinthians that their behavior may impact the way someone receives the gospel, but also leaves the statement that "So, whether you eat or drink, or whatever you do, do all to the glory of God."

How is 1 Corinthians 10:22-33 related to James' instructions in James 3:16-17?

Some people may feel a personal conviction or scruple to behave in a certain way. Personal convictions for ourselves are not the same as laws for others from the mouth of God. There are also some verses that require understanding of the culture to which they were written. A great example of this is 1 Timothy 2:9 where the instruction is given that women should not have braided hair and gold jewelry and pearls. Have you ever read that section of Scripture and wondered if God has something against braids?

What was the standard for physical appearance when you were a child? Were you told it was mandated by God?

What could be a current cultural comparison - something that may be considered taboo in your culture but isn't actually a Biblical mandate?

Let's think about James 2. If a woman walked into your church today and she had clothing with tons of designer labels, a very obviously expensive car, tons of expensive jewelry everywhere, and $3,000 shoes on, what would be people's reaction? Would she draw attention to herself instead of the Lord? Probably. However, if you braid your hair today, is anyone going to look at a French braid with a charm in it or a gorgeous set of locs with beads and ornaments and be unable to concentrate on the sermon? Probably not. We need to look at the initial intent of the author and read with cultural understanding.

The section of verses regarding appearance and behavior, 1 Timothy 2:8-10, says, "I desire then that in every place the men should pray, lifting holy hands without anger or quarreling; likewise also that women should adorn themselves in respectable apparel, with modesty an self-control, not with braided hair and gold or pearls or costly attire, but with what is proper for women who profess godliness - with good works."

The men are instructed to pray without anger or bickering, the women are told "likewise," which means "also," or "about the same thing," or "in the same way," the women should have self-control and not be showy, but focus on their behavior. Did you catch that? The men need to focus on their behavior and have the self control not to argue and the women need to focus on their behavior and internal heart to focus on the Lord and have the self control not to focus on appearance.

Have you found this to be something you struggle with? Remember that "...the Lord sees not as man sees: man looks on the outward appearance, but the Lord looks on the heart." (1 Samuel 16:7b)

The problem with reading the Bible without historical context and cultural understanding is that some churches have taken this literally. Women are not allowed to have braids, gold or pearls, etc, and it's mandated by churches. It's also been used to permit racial discrimination against Christians who use braids as part of normal hair styling and as protective hairstyles. Scan the QR code for more info.

It can be very difficult to discern between cultural norms and Biblical mandates if you were brought up in a culture that was very critical of physical appearance. If you were raised hearing criticisms of others' appearances voiced, or whispered behind hands as they left, it can be a hard habit to break, but it's necessary.

Have you ever been on the receiving end of judgement over your appearance? How did that make you feel about the group you were in? How does this experience add to your understanding of James' instructions in both Chapter 2 and 3 as discussed above?

To summarize, be sure that the behavior you are observing and making a judgement call on is actually biblically mandated and not your interpretation of it or your own personal convictions.

On a personal note, I keep struggling with whether these rabbit trail connections should be included in this study. One editor has advised me to remove them, but I've ignored her for a very specific reason: Bible study isn't linear, it's interconnected. Often, in order to gain fuller understanding, we have to pause, go check out a related Scripture, then come back to where we were.

I'm reminded that while this is a study on Hermeneutics and James,

"All Scripture is breathed out by God and profitable for teaching, for reproof, for correction, and for training in righteousness, that the man of God may be complete, equipped for every good work." (2 Timothy 3:16-17).

My desire for you is that you will leave this study with a greater understanding of who God is, how we should interact with Him and with others as believers, and that this study will help to equip you for future study and Christian life, as Paul wrote to Timothy above.

Part of Hermeneutics is understanding cultural context and the interconnectedness of the Bible, so I'm leaving it in and I hope it encourages you that study doesn't have to be restricted to one books the Bible at a time.

If you have notes or questions about this chapter, write them below for discussion.

CHAPTER 4

Before you begin, take a moment to pray and ask the Holy Spirit to open your mind and heart to know Him and understand His word. In the words of Paul, "that the God of our Lord Jesus Christ, the Father of glory, may give you the Spirit of wisdom and of revelation in the knowledge of him, having the eyes of your hearts enlightened, that you may know what is the hope to which he has called you…" (Ephesians 1:17-18). I encourage you to even insert your name into that verse and pray the scripture for yourself in this way:

Lord, I ask that the God of our Lord Jesus Christ, the Father of glory, will give me the Spirit of wisdom and revelation in the knowledge of Him. Please enlighten the eyes of my heart the I may know the hope to which you called me.

Read through all of Chapter 4, just to get a feel for it.
Below, write down themes that are repeated.

Read verses 1-11.
What does James say is one of the sources of conflict among believers?

How does this connect to James 1:13-15?

Verses 2-4 discuss one possible reason why what we ask of God may not be given to us. What is it?

Is it reasonable to use verses 2-4 when counseling others about unanswered prayer? Why or why not? Or in which situation would you or would you not share these verses?

Take a look at the context of this chapter. Remember that there were no chapter breaks in the original letter, so this section is just the next bit after Chapter 3, which was discussing wisdom and that our behaviors can show our priorities.

The next time someone comes to you and says, "God isn't answering my prayers, why isn't He?" Combine chapters 3 and 4 (and 1 for that matter). Pray and ask God for wisdom (1:13-15) so you know the correct way to answer; answer with meekness and humility (3:13), remembering that we don't know the mind of God.

Write down some advice you might give a friend who is in that situation, or use the scripture to give yourself Biblical advice.

Read verses 4-5, then read 1 John 2:15-17. What relationship to the world do James and John say is contrary to closeness with God?

Pause for a moment. Remind yourself of the truth of the scriptures. These verses are about relational closeness and continuing to grow in holiness. They are not about salvation. Read Ephesians 2:8-9. In the context of that verse, continue on to read the next section of verses, which contain little snippets of encouragement for how Christians should live, almost like reading sections of Proverbs.

Read verses 7-17 and underline (or list below) all of the verbs/verb phrases. Those are the actions or states of being, so you're looking for commands or actions. In the example below, "submit" is the verb, but I included the whole phrase "submit to God" for fuller information.

Submit to God

Based on Verse 6, where do we get the ability to do all of these behaviors that are listed through the rest of the chapter?

Why do you think verse 11, telling us not to speak evil of one another, comes after multiple verses telling us to humble ourselves before God and after entire chapters telling us to watch the behavior of others?

When we read verse 12, the command that we **don't** judge one another may seem contrary to other sections of the Bible wherein we are commanded **to** judge. How can we reconcile two seemingly contrary instructions?

Scan the code to the right and check out some of the definitions and situations in which the word "judge" is used in the New Testament.
On the next page, write some down.

How is G2919 ("judge") used in the New Testament?

Example1: Luke 7:43 Jesus says "you have judged rightly" in response to someone correctly interpreting scripture.

What is the conclusion you've come to about these instructions? How does the context of each verse affect the meaning/definition of what the verse is saying?

Now that we've looked at little more closely at that word, how does it impact your understanding of James 4:12-13?

Read verses 14-15.
How does the perspective in these verses differ from the "I'm going to live forever!" Attitude of the world in which we live?

If you truly lived each day with the expectation that the Lord could return today, or that each day might be your last, how would it change your choices, your behavior, and how you treat others?

Read verses 16-17.
What does James say about knowing the right thing to do and choosing not to do it?

CHAPTER 5

Before you begin, take a moment to pray and ask the Holy Spirit to open your mind and heart to know Him and understand His word. In the words of Paul, "that the God of our Lord Jesus Christ, the Father of glory, may give you the Spirit of wisdom and of revelation in the knowledge of him, having the eyes of your hearts enlightened, that you may know what is the hope to which he has called you…" (Ephesians 1:17-18). I encourage you to even insert your name into that verse and pray the scripture for yourself in this way:

Lord, I ask that the God of our Lord Jesus Christ, the Father of glory, will give me the Spirit of wisdom and revelation in the knowledge of Him. Please enlighten the eyes of my heart the I may know the hope to which you called me.

Read through all of Chapter 5, just to get a feel for it.
Below, write down themes that are repeated.

Read verses 1-6.
Write down your first impression of them below

In these six verses, James uses a lot of similes and metaphors to prove his point. Remember that both similes and metaphors compare one thing to another. Similes use 'like' or 'as' in their comparisons, metaphors say something 'is' or things 'are.' When he says things like 'your wealth has rotted' he isn't actually addressing piles of things they own that have rotted, he's addressing their value and their impact on the person who owns them.

With that understanding, what is James' message to the rich in these verses?

How do verses 1-5 relate to James 2:1-6?

Does this mean that God is against you if you are rich? No. However, Jesus said in Matthew 19:24, "Again I tell you, it is easier for a camel to go through the eye of a needle than for a rich person to enter the kingdom of God."

There's debate among scholars whether "the eye of a needle" is referring to an actual sewing needle, or a gate in Jerusalem. Scan the QR code for an article with more information.

Read Verses 7-9
When do these verses say that Christ is returning?

How can something be long enough off that we must patiently wait and also so near that Jesus is being described as "at the door"?

Think back to childhood. When you were left home alone by your parents, "I'll be back soon" is something you likely heard. Depending on your parent, that could have meant half an hour or hours. However, if you got a phone call saying "I'm on my way home," things were different. You'd start cleaning up, making sure things were in order, and generally preparing for the arrival of your parent.

This is the same - James is telling the church that while we don't know exactly the day or time of Christ's return, He **is** returning soon, so we should live with that mindset.

As a little side quest, read Matthew 24:36 and tuck it into your back pocket for the next time that you hear that a man has predicted the date of the return of Christ. It doesn't matter how good his math is or what is reasoning is, he's not going to supersede what is clearly stated in God's word.

Read Verses 10-11
What is James' expectation for the experiences believers will have during their lives?

How does the country and environment in which you were raised impact how you interact with people about sharing the gospel?

If you couldn't think of anything, consider this: the book of James was written in the first couple of decades after the death, resurrection, and ascension of Christ. The introduction says the letter is "to the twelve tribes scattered abroad" (James 1:1). This letter is written in light of those circumstances to instruct and encourage. How does that change your answer?

As you're finishing working through this study, do you have any lingering questions or ideas you need help working through?

PRAYER LIST/JOURNAL

For the eyes of the Lord are on the righteous,
and his ears are open to their prayer...
(1 Peter 3:12a)

Use this space to track what's on your mind and heart.

If you have trouble with anxiety or worry, I encourage you to use this section as a journal as well. Write down, in detail, what you are concerned about. Once you've written it down, mentally release it to God. "Mentally release it to God" is kind of a vague phrase, isn't it? How do you practically implement that?

> Application note: there is a difference between going through a difficult circumstance or having something weighing on your mind and clinical anxiety, depression, or religious OCD.
>
> Just as you would go to a doctor if you broke your leg or had an illness that needed medication, or were even just worried about a physical aspect of your health, it's ok to go to a doctor if your mind is the part of you that needs help. God has given these doctors the ability to analyze mental illness and provide support.
>
> Struggling with mental health is not evidence that you lack faith anymore than physical illness is.

Method 1: Verbally remind yourself of scriptural truth. An example of this would be praying the scripture like we do before beginning each day's study: "The eyes of the Lord are on the righteous and his ears are open to my prayer..." (1 Peter 3:12a) or "You have kept count of my wanderings; put my tears in your bottle. Are they not in your book?" (Psalm 56:8) or "In

58

peace I will both lie down and sleep; for you alone, O Lord, make me dwell in safety." (Psalm 4:8)

Method 2: Pray about it. God is a loving father who isn't bothered by hearing from you. If you have a concern you can't get out of your mind, tell God you're focusing on it and need help with releasing it.

Method 3: Go do something else. Choose something active and useful or relaxing and calming, depending on what you need.

Method 4: Ask a close friend to pray for you and with you. I'd encourage you to not broadcast struggles on social media, no matter how tempting it may be. Social media is no replacement for person-to-person contact.

Make yourself a plan right now for how you'll address these situations the next time they come up. When we're stuck in a spiral of anxiety or worry, critical thinking isn't our strong suit. Having a plan before the problem arises releases you from the burden of trying to figure things out when the situation is intense.

QUESTIONS AND ANSWERS

Use this space to write down questions that you think of as you're working through the study. Don't just ignore them - write them down and search for answers! If you can't find answers on your own, make sure you ask someone else for help. The answers do exist!

_____

_____

_____

_____

_____

_____

_____

_____

_____

_____

_____

_____

_____

_____

_____

_____

_____

_____

_____

_____

_____

_____

_____

Bibliography

Bible Hub. "Paul's Missionary Journeys." ISV. Accessed January 10, 2026. https://biblehub.com/atlas/isv/paul.jpg

Cheng, Brian. "'Deus in Machina': Swiss church installs AI Jesus to connect the digital and the divine" NBC. December 5, 2024. https://www.nbcnews.com/news/world/deus-machina-swiss-church-installs-ai-jesus-connect-digital-divine-rcna182973

Christian Book Distributors. Accessed December 28, 2025. https://www.christianbook.com/page/bibles/about-bibles/bible-translation-reading-levels?

Christian Book Distributors. Accessed December 28, 2025. https://www.christianbook.com/page/bibles/about-bibles/about-translations?event=Bibles|1005256

CSB Holy Land Illustrated Bible (Nashville, Tennessee: Holman Bible Publishers, 2020) 1794.

Grammarly. "What Is a Noun? Definition, Types, and Examples" January 24, 2025. https://www.grammarly.com/blog/parts-of-speech/nouns/

Hinton, Clara. "ChatGPT in the pulpit: Meet the OKC pastor using AI as a tool in preparing his sermons." The Oklahoman. July 20, 2025. https://www.yahoo.com/news/chatgpt-pulpit-meet-okc-pastor-104549360.html

Jenkins, Jack. "Charlie Kirk's AI Resurrection Ushers in a New Era of Digital Grief" Church Leaders. September 18, 2024. https://churchleaders.com/news/1108715-charlie-kirks-ai-resurrection-digital-grief-rns.html

Lyle, Linda. "Camel through the Eye of a Needle? What Did Jesus Mean in Matt. 19:24?" Bible Study Tools. September 18, 2025. https://www.biblestudytools.com/bible-study/topical-studies/camel-through-the-eye-of-a-needle-what-did-jesus-mean-in-matt-1924.html

Ortiz, Kenneth. "Christian History Timeline: Most Influential Events in Church History." February 23, 2023. https://www.theologyfortherestofus.com/christian-history-timeline-most-influential-events-in-church-history#aa

Salvadore, Sarah. "Catholic schools slow to accept cultural significance of black hair" National Catholic Review. February 20, 2020. https://www.ncronline.org/news/catholic-schools-slow-accept-cultural-significance-black-hair

Shakespeare, William. "Romeo and Juliet." MIT. Accessed January 2, 2026.http://shakespeare.mit.edu/romeo_juliet/full.html

The National Literacy Institute. Accessed December 24, 2025. https://www.thenationalliteracyinstitute.com/2024-2025-literacy-statistics.

Wordnik. Accessed December 31, 2025. https://www.wordnik.com/words/metaphor